Foreword

"But everyone does it these days; surely it's the best way to find out if we are really compatible before we make the decision to marry." We have all heard these opinions in defence of cohabitation.

Many people today feel they need to 'try out' their partner before committing themselves to marriage. Others no longer see any point in getting married at all, especially when faced with the astronomical cost of a wedding and the evidence of divorce all around them. So are we out of date as Christians to be concerned about this change of attitude towards cohabitation and marriage? Should we just keep our heads down and hope that marriage will come back into vogue some time in the future?

It is to address this very issue that two such qualified people, who I respect and admire, have written this Report. Declan Flanagan is a long standing friend, and I know him to be passionate about the Truth. Ted Williams is an experienced medical practitioner and a specialist in public health medicine.

Declan and Ted have not kept their heads down and ignored the issue of widespread cohabitation. Instead they have tackled the issue head on. In this timely and well argued Report they help us understand the full implications of cohabitation, enabling us to deal with the issue amongst our family, friends, colleagues and congregations in a sensitive and thoughtful way.

Cohabitation or Marriage? is an extremely informative resource that you can readily use to persuade and convince others of the benefits of marriage. It is written with compassion and ends on a note of hope, reminding us that the Christian gospel is about forgiveness and redemption. I commend it to your reading and am sure you will pass it's message on!

LYNDON BOWRING
EXECUTIVE CHAIRMAN, CARE

Contents

	page
1. Introduction	3
2. Trends in cohabitation	4
2.1 Premarital cohabitation	4
2.2 Prevalence of cohabitation	4
2.3 Duration of cohabitation	4
3. Debate in the Church of England	5
3.1 Why the Church cannot remain silent	6
4. Arguments in favour of cohabitation	7
4.1 Trial marriage	7
4.2 Marriage is outdated	7
5. God's plan for marriage	9
5.1 He created them male and female	10
5.2 A man will be united to his wife	10
5.3 Two become one flesh	11
5.4 What God has joined together let no man separate	13
6. Dangers of cohabitation	15
6.1 Cohabitation and divorce	15
6.2 Smoking	17
6.3 Infant mortality	18
6.4 Sexual behaviour	18
6.5 Abortion	20
6.6 Venereal disease	21
6.7 Neurotic disorders	21
7. Conclusion	24
7.1 The Church needs to warn society	24
7.2 An invitation to a better way	25
7.3 Good news for those who cohabit	26
Bibliography	27
Acknowledgments	28

1. Introduction

A major social trend of the last three decades is the decline in marriage and the rise in cohabitation. Over the last twenty years, the number of marriages has fallen considerably, while there has been a growth in the number of couples living together without marrying. In 1993 the number of marriages in the UK fell to its lowest level for 50 years and one in five unmarried men and women were cohabiting. The stigma attached to cohabiting in the 1990s is far less than it was two or three decades ago. Consequently many couples are content to live together, some regarding their relationship as a 'trial marriage'. Others reject the institution of marriage and never plan to wed. Cohabitation is now socially acceptable, although it is contrary to the most fundamental teachings of the Christian faith. This acceptance by society is, perhaps, best shown by the way language has changed – the term 'partner' is now in common use. Contemporary society seldom distinguishes between cohabiting partners and married couples.

"Living together before marriage has become the practice of an increasing majority... Trends suggest that the proportion cohabiting will tend to increase whilst the proportion married will decline"

JOHN HASKEY
POPULAR TRENDS

2. Trends in cohabitation

Key Points in marriage trends

The number of first marriages in 1993 was the lowest recorded this century.

Since 1970 there has been a steep decline in marriage rates for men and women under 30.

The proportion of marriages solemnised in church has decreased from 84% at the turn of the century to 50% in 1993.

Recent statistics show that 38% of marriages involved the remarriage of one or both partners.

2.1 Premarital cohabitation

The trend in premarital cohabitation is illustrated in figure 1. It shows that in the mid-1960s around 5% of single women lived with their future husband before marriage. By the 1990s about 70% were cohabiting prior to marriage. Of women marrying a second time in the 1990s, about 90% will cohabit before their second marriage.

2.2 Prevalence of cohabitation

Prevalence refers to the proportion of people in society cohabiting at a particular point in time. The proportion of single women cohabiting in 1979 was 7.5%, and this had more than trebled to 23% by 1993. Divorced men have the highest rate of cohabitation – in 1993 over 40% were in such a relationship. Taking all unmarried people together, over one in five were cohabiting in 1993 compared to one in seven in the mid-1980s.

2.3 Duration of cohabitation

The General Household Survey provides information on the length of cohabitation. Of course the durations measured in this way are incomplete, for it is not known at the time of interview how long each current spell of cohabitation will last. Nevertheless, the calculated durations do give an indication of trends. At the time they were interviewed, 34% of cohabiting single women had been in their relationship for less than 18 months. The average length of cohabitation for single women increased from 19 months in 1986 to 29 months in 1993.

3. Debate in the Church of England

The rise in the prevalence of cohabitation has led to a major debate in the Church of England and a report commissioned by the Synod entitled **Something to Celebrate** gave guarded approval to cohabitation. According to the report, some cohabiting relationships are marriages in all but name, so the label "living in sin" is no longer appropriate. The Archbishop of Canterbury, however, expressed disappointment that the report did not maintain a clear focus on the biblical ideals embodied in family life and society. The Archbishop stated, "the wisdom and truth of the Christian tradition are that a married man and woman and their children should be the basic building block of family life. Cohabitation is not, and cannot be, marriage in all but name. Those who choose to cohabit on the grounds that their relationship is a private matter and nothing to do with the wider society are, frankly, deluding themselves. Marriage, not cohabitation, is the institution that is at the heart of a good society, and let us not be reluctant to say so. I do not say this in condemnation; I say it as an invitation to a better way."

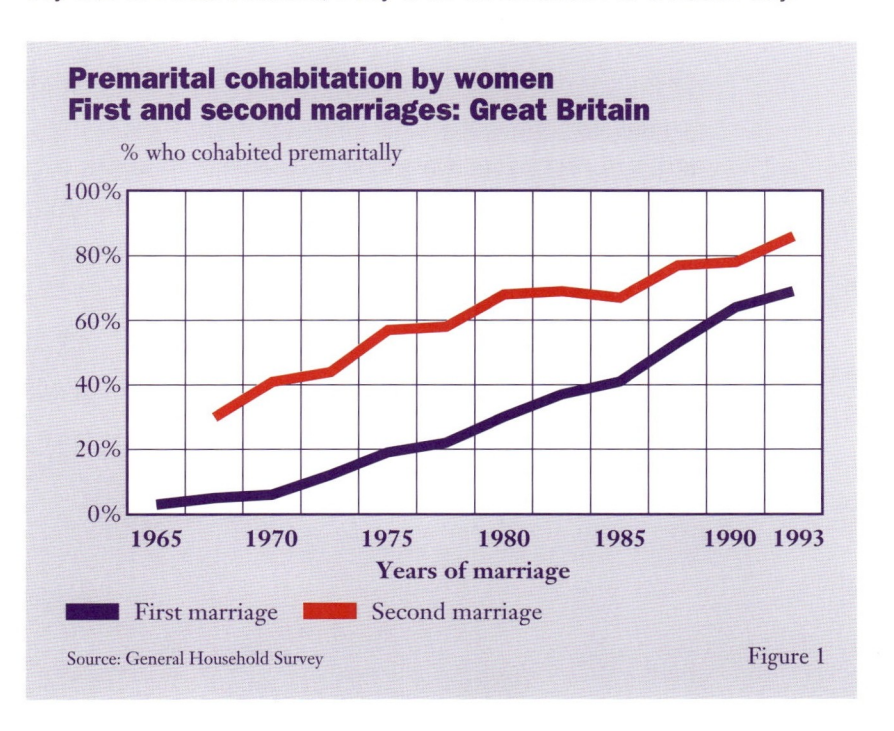

> *"The wisdom and truth of the Christian tradition are that a married man and woman and their children should be the basic building block of family life... Marriage, not cohabitation, is the institution that is at the heart of a good society and let us not be reluctant to say so."*
>
> ARCHBISHOP DR GEORGE CAREY

Premarital cohabitation by women
First and second marriages: Great Britain

% who cohabited premaritally, by Years of marriage (1965–1993), First marriage and Second marriage.

Source: General Household Survey

Figure 1

3. Debate in the Church of England

3.1 Why the Church cannot remain silent

The Archbishop's comments are encouraging, for he has felt the need to speak out against the move towards widespread cohabitation. Yet the popular view is that it is judgmental to comment on moral issues and few people have felt inclined to do so. The right of individual people to set their own moral standards without interference from others is regarded as sacrosanct. All are free to do what they think is right in their own eyes, without reference to the moral standards set out in the Bible. The Christian view of marriage is under constant challenge – the point has been reached in the United Kingdom where most couples cohabit before marriage and the Church has little to say on the subject.

> *"For many couples there is a mixture of attitudes to, and reasons for, living together rather than marrying, as undoubtedly there is a variety of opinions about the advisability of doing so"*
>
> JOHN HASKEY
> POPULAR TRENDS

The Christian Church, however, must not remain silent. It has an obligation to enter the debate by reaffirming the biblical standards of marriage. It is necessary for the Church to speak prophetically, warning of the devastating consequences of disobeying God's word for both the individual and society. *God's wrath comes on those who are disobedient* (Ephesians 5:6). *God cannot be mocked. A man reaps what he sows. The one who sows to please his sinful nature, from that nature will reap destruction* (Galatians 6:7). Failure to speak out marginalises the Church and weakens its witness. When God's way is upheld, it is for the good of all. However, when God's law is rejected, then all society will bear the consequences.

The purpose of this report is, first, to examine what the Bible says about marriage and cohabitation and, second, to present information on the social and health consequences of cohabitation.

4. Arguments in favour of cohabitation

Cohabitation is defined as a relationship in which a man and a woman live together and regularly engage in sexual intercourse without being married. Two major arguments are put forward by those who advocate cohabitation. The first is that it is wise for a couple to live together before getting married, so that they can have a trial period in which to confirm their compatibility. This view supports the idea of premarital cohabitation. The second argument is that marriage is an outdated institution which needs to be replaced by cohabitation.

4.1 Trial marriage

The first position is held by people who do not oppose marriage as such but are nervous of entering into an unhappy marriage. They consider that it is necessary to live together before marriage to test their compatibility and commitment to each other. Should the trial not succeed then it is easy to end the relationship and move on to the next one without experiencing the trauma of the divorce courts.

"For those cohabiting a much higher proportion report two or more partners in the last year than do married people... This may in turn reflect either the less committed nature of cohabiting relationships or the more liberal attitudes of cohabitees towards non-exclusive relationships."

SEXUAL ATTITUDES AND LIFESTYLES

It is commonly believed that 'trial marriage' reduces the likelihood of a marriage breaking down. Later in this report we will show that those who cohabit before marriage actually increase the probability of divorce.

4.2 Marriage is outdated

The second argument is advanced by those who believe that marriage is no longer relevant in a modern world. It is said to be restrictive and oppressive, limiting the freedom of individuals to express themselves. The marriage relationship is seen as a means of reinforcing sexual stereotypes and exploiting women.

4. Arguments in favour of cohabitation

> *"The essence of sexual immorality is that a man and a woman seek physical and emotional satisfaction from each other, but have not made a permanent commitment to each other. The pleasure that they obtain in this way is stolen. They have not paid the due price for it"*
>
> **DEREK PRINCE**

According to High Court Judge Brenda Hoggett, one of the authors of the Law Commission's 1990 report on family law, "Logically, we have already reached a point at which ... we should be considering whether the legal institution of marriage continues to serve any useful purpose." Cohabiting, on the other hand, allows greater freedom, offering the sexual and emotional closeness of marriage while retaining the autonomy of singleness. Cohabiting partners are independent individuals who enjoy freedom from the gender roles inherent in the husband/wife relationship. Cohabitation is thought to enable couples to live with each other free from the restrictions imposed by outdated marriage vows. Moreover it is easy, convenient, and socially accepted by modern society. So, if two people are in love, it is quite proper for them to live together. Those who hold such views see no reason ever to get married, and rather choose cohabitation. An essential aim of cohabitation is that each partner should achieve self-fulfilment. When either partner is no longer satisfied by the relationship, he or she is free to seek self-fulfilment elsewhere.

5. God's plan for marriage

Many people see little difference between marriage and cohabitation. Indeed, as we have already seen, some argue that cohabitation is marriage in all but name. So there is confusion in contemporary society about what constitutes marriage, and many people see no purpose in an expensive marriage ceremony and attach little value to a marriage certificate. Hence the question frequently arises, "Why bother with marriage? After all, what difference can a marriage certificate make?" In today's world there is almost no appreciation of the biblical view of marriage.

> "Marriage is not a thing ordained by men. We know that God is the author of it and that it is solemnised in his name. The Scripture says that it is a holy covenant, and therefore calls it divine."
>
> JOHN CALVIN

The biblical foundation of marriage is provided in the first two chapters of the Bible, which give an account of the creation of the heavens and the earth, and the creation of man in the image of God. It is significant that marriage is established from the beginning of God's dealing with the human race. Eve is referred to as the wife of Adam in the second chapter of Genesis. The biblical basis is laid in two key verses from Genesis.

God created man in his own image; male and female he created them. God blessed them and said to them, "Be fruitful and increase in number..." (Genesis 1: 27-28). *For this reason a man will leave his father and mother and be united to his wife, and they will become one flesh* (Genesis 2: 24).

With these words in the first chapters of the Bible, God established the basic principles for marriage and procreation. Marriage is the institution established by God for the fulfilment of the command to be fruitful and for the purpose of companionship between men and women. Jesus refers to the verses from Genesis quoted above to teach the basis of marriage and goes on to say,

5. God's plan for marriage

"So they are no longer two, but one. Therefore what God has joined together, let man not separate" (Matthew 19: 4-6). So Jesus endorsed marriage as a divine ordinance and drew attention to its four essential characteristics.

5.1 He created them male and female

God, in creating human beings in His own image, created them male and female, by design. Marriage is the Creator's plan for the coming together of one man and one woman in an exclusive sexual union. Marriage is a heterosexual union, confined to two people only. Sexual union between a man and a woman is necessary to produce children and thereby fulfil God's command to be fruitful.

5.2 A man will be united to his wife

Leaving one family to form another is at the heart of marriage. It becomes known in the community that the man and woman have left their parents and now live together as a new family. They have committed themselves to each other and are not available to anyone else. That is the secure environment into which children, if the marriage is fruitful, are to be born, nurtured and allowed to develop into mature adults. One of the most important features of marriage is that it is a public event which takes place before witnesses, so acknowledging that others in society are involved. Marriage is not a private partnership between two people – it is the building block of society and so affects others in the community.

> *"The event the Bible calls marriage involved the whole society. The idea of a purely private marriage is simply a recent aberration, the result of individualism and of the disintegration of traditional communities. The marriage feast assured that the marriage was a public event."*
>
> HENRI BLOCHER

COHABITATION OR MARRIAGE?

5. God's plan for marriage

Marriages need the support of other people and, in turn, strong marriages bring great benefit to society as a whole. Cohabitation, however, is a private arrangement made between two people and often disregards the wishes of others.

A man is to be united to his wife. The lifelong union of a man and a woman, expressed by promises made in public, is an essential feature of marriage. It contains the solemn promise to remain faithful. Marriage is a commitment made despite difficulties that may arise. In contrast, those who choose to cohabit have made no public promises of commitment to one another. It is not surprising, therefore, that cohabitation is so often a relatively short-lived arrangement.

5.3 Two become one flesh

Christ refers to Genesis 2:24, *"the two will become one flesh,"* and draws the conclusion *"So they are no longer two, but one"* (Matthew 19:6). The phrase 'one flesh' clearly refers to sexual intercourse which consummates the marriage. The order of his words indicate that the sexual union follows the 'leaving' and 'uniting'. The final proof of the uniting of the man and woman is sexual intercourse, which consummates the marriage and enables husband and wife to fulfil the divine command to be fruitful and multiply. Having children is one of the main purposes of marriage, and husband and wife readily accept that their sexual relationship may lead to the birth of children, and so enlarge their family. Cohabitation, on the other hand, allows sexual union on a trial basis.

> *"Marriage is an exclusive heterosexual covenant between one man and one woman, ordained and sealed by God, preceded by a public leaving of parents, consummated by sexual union, issuing in a permanent mutually supportive partnership, and normally crowned by the gift of children."*
>
> JOHN STOTT

5. God's plan for marriage

> *"The great fault of premarital sexual intercourse is quite simply that it demands privilege without responsibility; it demands rights without commitment. That is why sexual intercourse is wrong even between people who say that they are in love and that marriage is certain."*
>
> WILLIAM BARCLAY

If things do not work out, the relationship is ended; sexual union is not founded in total commitment, and many cohabiting couples are not prepared to accept children who may be the natural result of their sexual relationship. This may be the reason why cohabitation is associated with high rates of abortion, as we shall see later in this report.

However, there is more to the 'one flesh' idea than sexual intercourse. The conclusion of Jesus; *"So they are no longer two, but one"* stresses that at marriage a profound union takes place. A husband and wife become one entity – a new family of which God is the author. The custom of a woman taking the last name of the man she marries symbolises their 'oneness' as husband and wife. From the time of marriage the wife and any children who are born into the family are known by the family name. Furthermore, through marriage the husband and wife become members of a wider extended family, with a host of new family relationships. Both husband and wife may acquire many relatives, which may include a father and mother-in-law, and brother and sister-in-law. With a cohabiting arrangement there is no true 'oneness', and the cohabiting couple each retain their own names, thereby emphasising that they are indeed two separate individuals. No new family relationships are created and the wishes of parents and other family members are often not considered, illustrating the self-centred nature of the arrangement.

The values propounded by secular thinking have promoted a casual approach to sexual relationships. It is acceptable to enter such a relationship without commitment in the pursuit of pleasure. Yet there is no more intimate connection possible between two people. It has the potential that no other physical act contains – it evokes powerful emotions, and may result in the woman becoming pregnant.

Many people believe that no harm results from a series of cohabitations, provided there is honesty between partners. This is a delusion, for few people survive multiple cohabitations without feeling that they have devalued themselves, and without suffering emotional trauma. This is because God has designed the sex act to be a loving expression of commitment to another person. When sexual intercourse takes place in a casual relationship, its meaning is devalued and it demeans those who participate. In particular, women who participate in a casual sexual relationship are liable to feel that they have been used to gratify the sexual lust of another person. It is not surprising that many women who become pregnant in cohabiting relationships are deserted by their partners.

Some people portray the Christian faith as being anti-sex. Nothing could be further from the truth. The Song of Solomon vividly describes a high view of the relationship between a man and a woman, characterised by sexual love. The Song speaks profoundly of the beauty and delights of love expressed in an exclusive relationship. *"My lover is mine and I am his"* (Song of Solomon 2: 16).

5.4 What God has joined together let no man separate

This is the command that Jesus made to emphasise the permanence of marriage. When he was questioned about the reasons for divorce, he quoted the two verses from Genesis mentioned above and then emphasised that those who marry are joined by God and so should not be separated by other people. When a man and a woman are joined in marriage, they are obeying God's law and are joined together as husband and wife. The union is permanent and the married couple should not separate – marriage is for life. So marriage is a serious undertaking which is to provide security for any children who may result. For these reasons other people must not attempt to destroy a marriage, and marriage partners must not allow any relationship to develop that endangers it.

5. God's plan for marriage

> "Sexual intercourse is essentially bound up with marriage. It is therefore appropriate only within marriage. Sex outside of marriage becomes a serious moral issue only because marriage is of enormous importance to the human family and the future God has for his people."
>
> LEWIS SMEDES

Jesus said that marital unfaithfulness is to be avoided at all costs, for it constitutes grounds for divorce. Cohabitation, as we shall see later, is not characterised by faithfulness to one partner. Indeed, it is usually a temporary union which cannot be obedient to the marriage ordinance, and is not pleasing to God.

In summary, God's plan for a successful marriage is that it should be an exclusive sexual relationship with one person, for life. This will require faithfulness as well as the mutual responsibilities of submission and love. Unfortunately, because of the frailty of human nature there are many marriages that are less than perfect. Indeed, some end in acrimony and divorce because marriage partners do not try to follow the biblical principles outlined above. This does not mean that the principles of marriage are wrong, but rather that the hearts of men and women are hard and do not readily accept God's way.

6. Dangers of cohabitation

If the biblical basis for marriage as described above is valid, and if marriage is God's intended way for couples to live together in a sexual relationship, then we would expect that those who follow God's way will reap the benefits, and that those who do not will suffer the consequences. All actions have consequences, and cohabitation is no exception. In this section we will examine some associated social and health implications.

6.1   Cohabitation and divorce

One of the main arguments in favour of couples living together before marriage is that it allows them a trial period in which to confirm their compatibility and commitment and so avoid an unhappy marriage. These so called 'trial marriages' are supposed to reduce the likelihood of future divorce. Yet an examination of the facts shows the converse to be true. Data from the General Household Survey shows that a couple who cohabit before marriage are, on average, twice as likely to divorce as a couple who do not cohabit before marriage. For example, among women aged between 40 and 50 who married when they were in their early twenties (20-24) and who cohabited before marriage, 39% were divorced compared to 21% of those who did not. Taking all age groups, the ratio of divorce between couples who premaritally cohabited and couples who did not cohabit, is 1.8 to 1, showing an 80% greater likelihood of divorce among those who cohabited before marriage.

Information collected by the General Household Survey allows divorce rates by duration of marriage to be estimated for couples in their first marriage. From this data the probability of a marriage ending in divorce or separation can be calculated for both those who cohabited premaritally and those who did not. The higher probability of marital breakdown among those who cohabited before their marriage is clearly illustrated in figure 2. According to an article in Population

6. Dangers of cohabitation

Trends the results are clear cut: "For every duration of marriage, the cumulative proportions of marriages which had broken down are higher amongst marriages in which there was premarital cohabitation than amongst marriages in which there was no premarital cohabitation."

Among those divorced, the prevalence of cohabiting before a second marriage has always been higher than before a first marriage. The older the man or woman, the greater the proportion who cohabit premaritally before their second marriage. The idea that premarital cohabitation reduces the likelihood of an unhappy marriage is false.

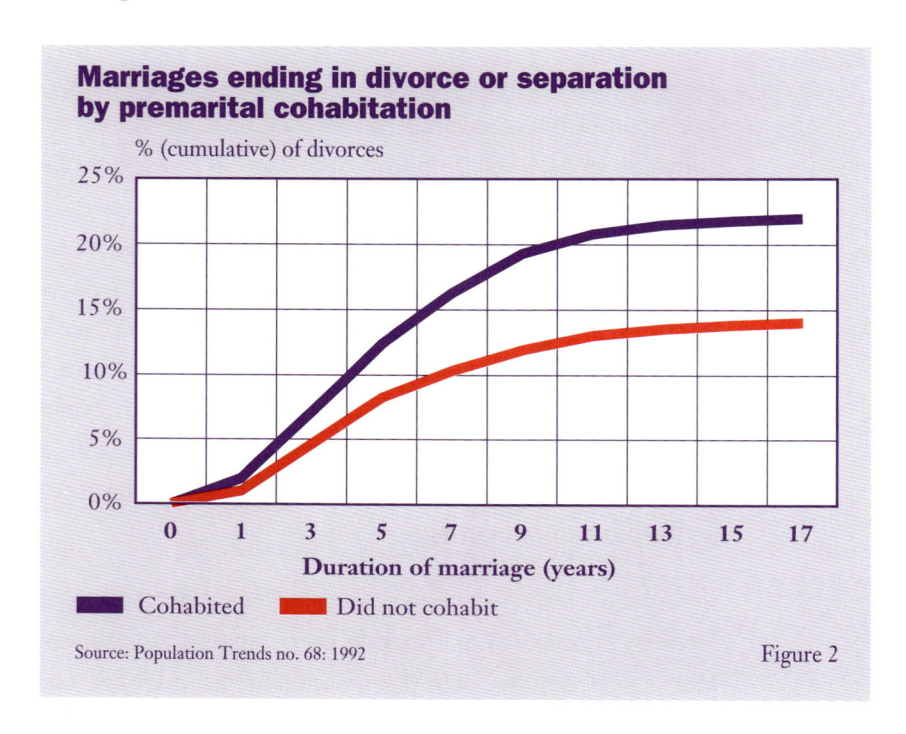

Marriages ending in divorce or separation by premarital cohabitation

Cohabited — Did not cohabit

Source: Population Trends no. 68: 1992

Figure 2

6.2   Smoking

Figure 3 shows smoking during pregnancy by marital status. Observe the large difference in smoking behaviour, with the proportion of cohabiting and single mothers who smoke being more than double that of married mothers. What is significant is that the smoking behaviour of cohabiting mothers (who have partners) resembles that of single mothers (who do not have partners) rather than that of married mothers. This suggests that cohabiting mothers have more in common with single mothers than their married counterparts. So why do so many cohabiting mothers smoke during their pregnancy? An important contributing factor is likely to be the stress and insecurity they feel in their relationship. It is predictable, then, that the babies of cohabiting mothers are more likely to be classified as low birthweight (under 2500 grammes) than babies born to married mothers (8.8% and 6.8% respectively).

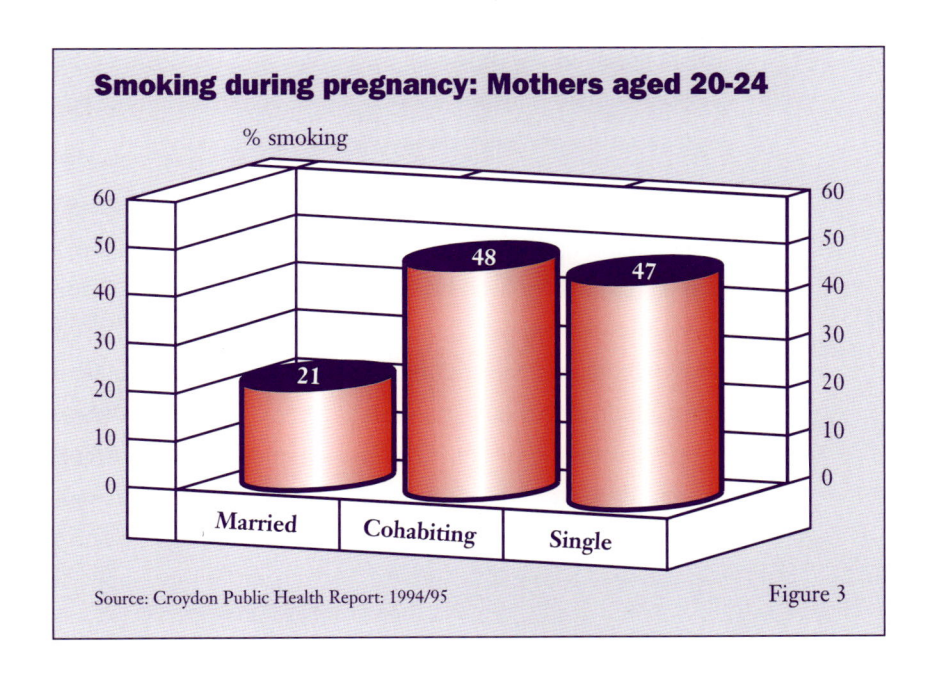

Smoking during pregnancy: Mothers aged 20-24

% smoking

- Married: 21
- Cohabiting: 48
- Single: 47

Source: Croydon Public Health Report: 1994/95

Figure 3

6. Dangers of cohabitation

6.3 Infant mortality

Infant mortality (the death of a baby in the first year of life) is widely recognised as one of the best indicators of infant health in a community. National figures on infant mortality for the period 1988 to 1990 show wide variations in death rates between babies born inside and outside marriage. Parents who are not married but give the same address when they registered the baby are assumed to be in a cohabiting relationship. The death rate for babies born to parents in a cohabiting relationship (9.8 per 1000 live births) is 35% higher than that of babies born to married parents (7.3 per 1000 live births). The infant mortality rates for babies born to single mothers (13.1) is even higher. This data suggests that babies born to cohabiting and single parents are at greater risk of ill-health than babies born within marriage.

6.4 Sexual behaviour

The national survey of sexual behaviour, which collected data from a random sample of nearly 19,000 representatives of British society, is the largest survey of sexual behaviour conducted in the UK.

Patterns of sexual behaviour in the last five years for men and women by marital status are described in figures 4 and 5. They show the proportion of men and women who have been monogamous (one sexual partner during the last five years), serially monogamous (a new sexual relationship after another has finished) or have had concurrent sexual partners (a new sexual relationship during an existing one). The figures show that married people are far more likely to be monogamous than the other marital groups. Well over 90% of married women have been monogamous during the last five years, compared to around 60% of women who were cohabiting.

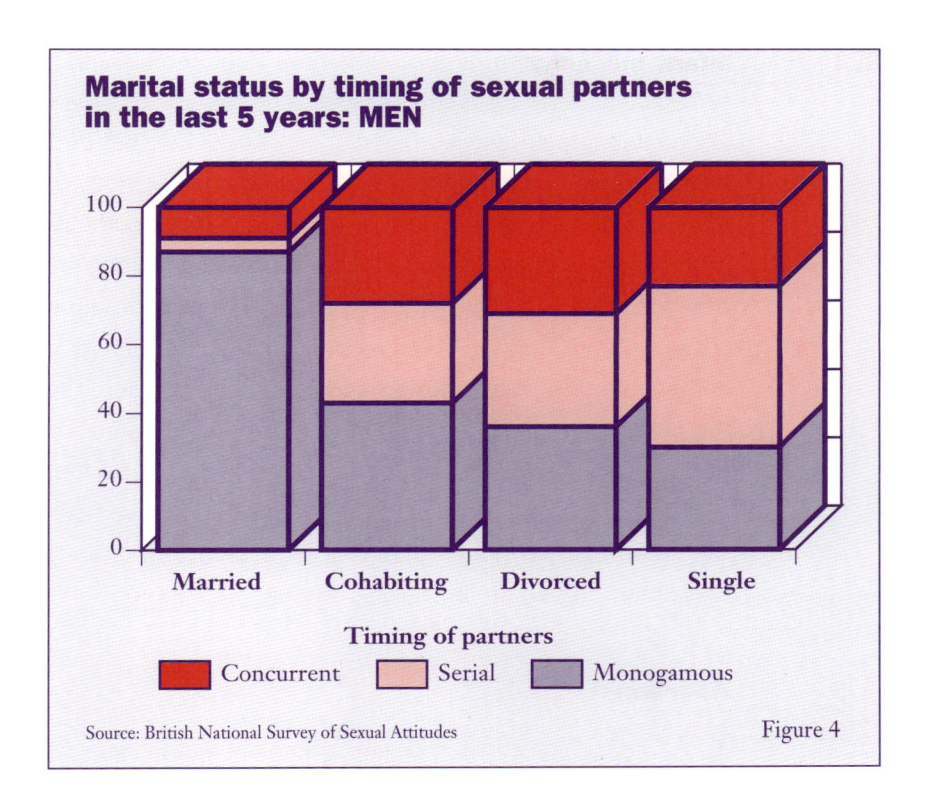

Marital status by timing of sexual partners in the last 5 years: MEN

Timing of partners: Concurrent, Serial, Monogamous

Source: British National Survey of Sexual Attitudes

Figure 4

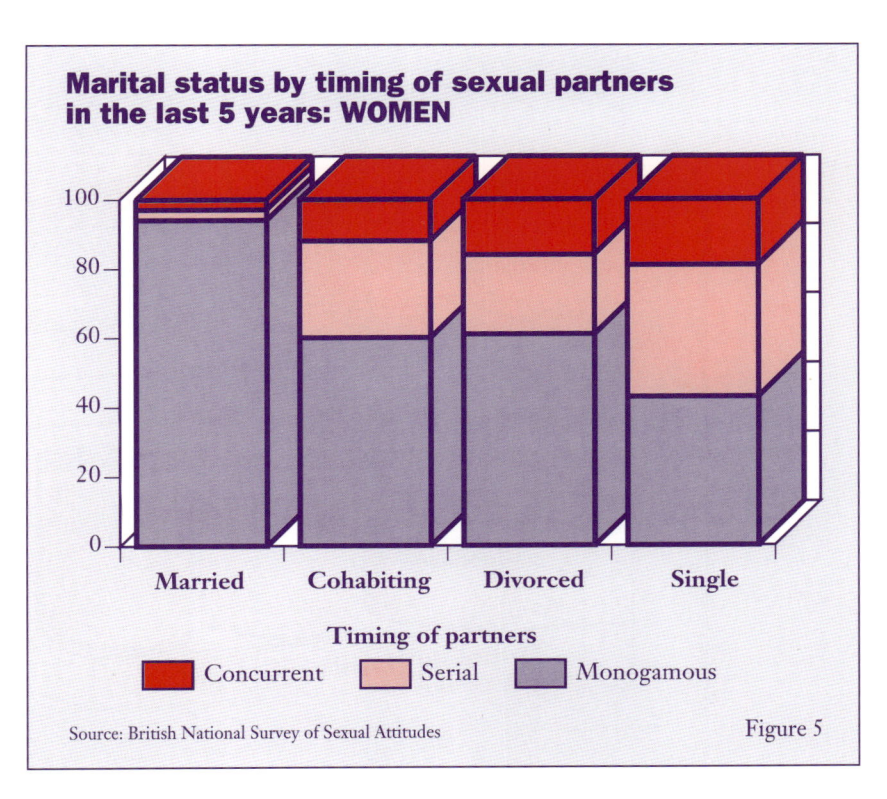

Marital status by timing of sexual partners in the last 5 years: WOMEN

Timing of partners: Concurrent, Serial, Monogamous

Source: British National Survey of Sexual Attitudes

Figure 5

6. Dangers of cohabitation

Among married men, around 90% have been monogamous, compared to 43% of cohabiting men. Moreover, the pattern of sexual behaviour of cohabiting men and women closely resembles that of divorced and single people. According to Sexual Attitudes and Lifestyle, "The influence of living with a partner as a measure of commitment to a relationship is unclear, since those who are cohabiting show patterns that are more like those who are single, divorced or separated than those who are married". These findings indicate a major difference in commitment between married and cohabiting couples. Undeniably, the majority of cohabiting relationships are associated with a pattern of behaviour that lacks commitment to one sexual partner. The vast majority of married couples, on the other hand, have been faithful to their marriage partners – disproving the assertion often made that most married people are having affairs.

6.5 Abortion

It is not well known that cohabiting is associated with high rates of legal abortion. Figure 6 shows the proportion of women reporting an abortion in the last five years. Abortion is least common among the

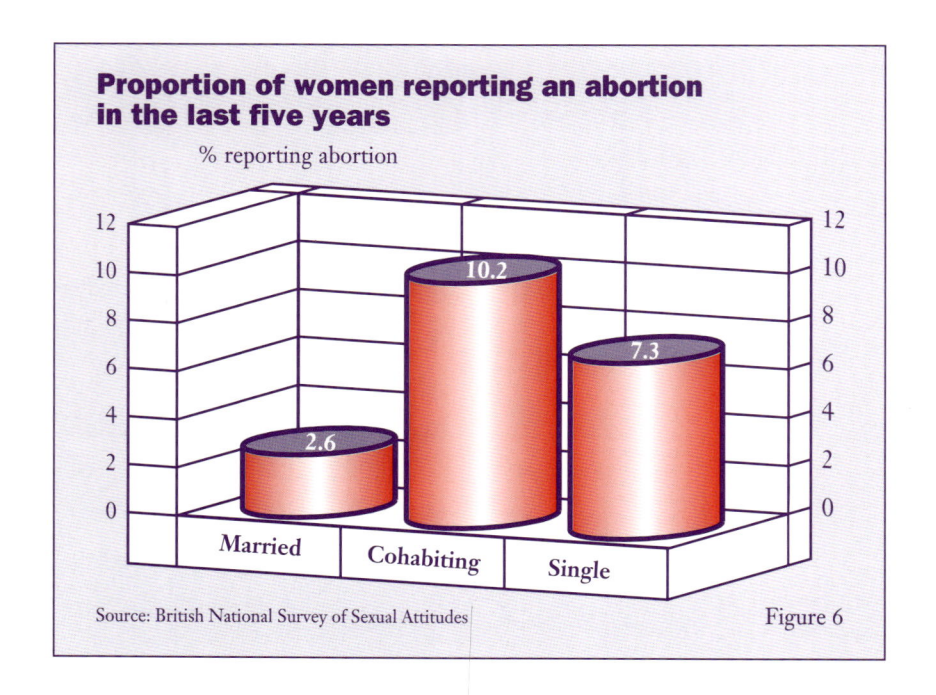

Proportion of women reporting an abortion in the last five years

% reporting abortion

- Married: 2.6
- Cohabiting: 10.2
- Single: 7.3

Source: British National Survey of Sexual Attitudes

Figure 6

widowed (1.2%) and married (2.6%); single women reported higher rates (7.3%), but the highest rates were among cohabiting women (10.2%). This finding is consistent with the less monogamous lifestyle of those people who cohabit. It appears that while they are prepared to live together in a sexual relationship, they are less committed to raising a family together.

6.6 Venereal disease

We have already seen that cohabiting is often associated with multiple sexual partners. It is usually accepted that attendance at special treatment disease clinics is a proxy measure for the incidences of venereal disease. The national survey shows that 6.3% of cohabiting women have attended such a clinic in the last five years compared to 1.1% of married women, suggesting that cohabiting women have higher rates of venereal disease.

6.7 Neurotic disorders

A large national survey of mental illness was commissioned by the Department of Health. The aim was to provide information about the prevalence of psychiatric problems among adults, aged between 16 and 64, in Great Britain. The level of neurotic symptoms in society was measured by a well validated questionnaire called the Clinical Interview Schedule. The Schedule is made up of fourteen sections, each covering a particular area of neurotic symptoms, such as worry, irritability, depression and anxiety. The overall threshold for significant psychiatric illness was a score of 12. Information for the survey was collected by 200 trained interviewers visiting a scientifically chosen sample of 10,000 British households. The findings of the survey, published in 1995, showed large and significant differences in neurotic behaviour between married, cohabiting and single groups. The overall prevalence of neurotic symptoms, as measured by the Interview Schedule, is shown in figure 7.

6. Dangers of cohabitation

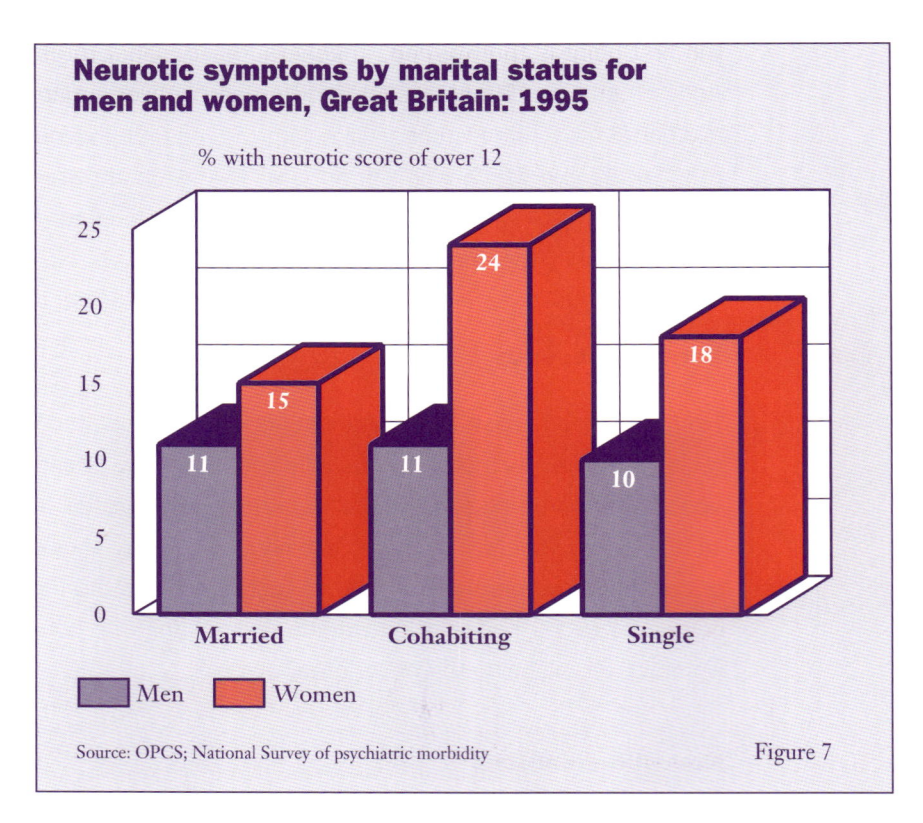

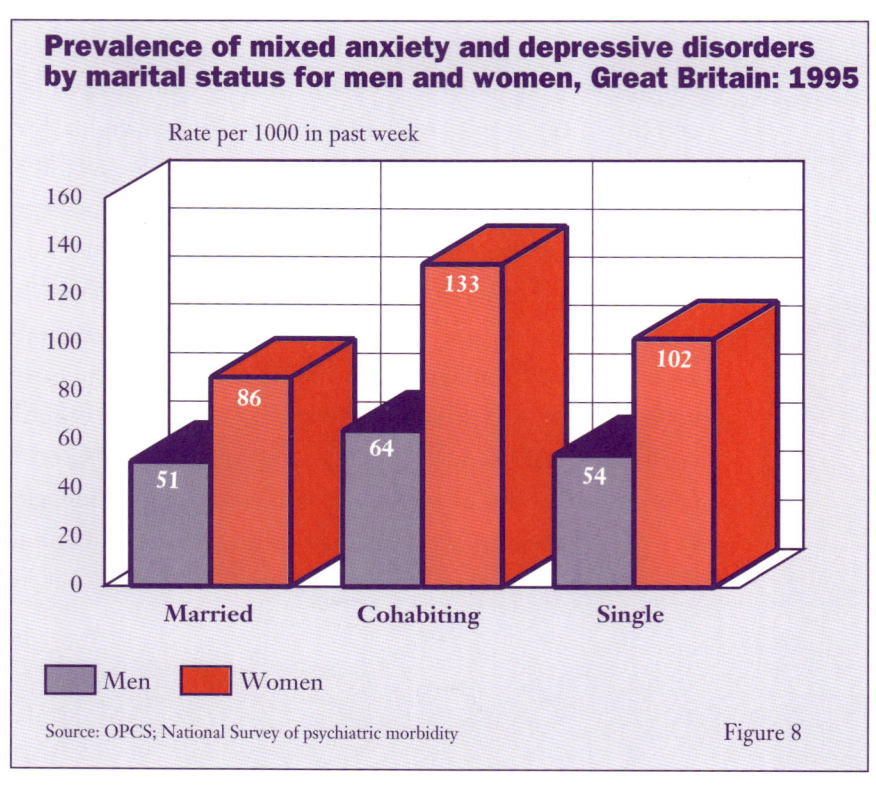

Neurotic symptoms by marital status for men and women, Great Britain: 1995

% with neurotic score of over 12

	Men	Women
Married	11	15
Cohabiting	11	24
Single	10	18

Source: OPCS; National Survey of psychiatric morbidity

Figure 7

Prevalence of mixed anxiety and depressive disorders by marital status for men and women, Great Britain: 1995

Rate per 1000 in past week

	Men	Women
Married	51	86
Cohabiting	64	133
Single	54	102

Source: OPCS; National Survey of psychiatric morbidity

Figure 8

6. Dangers of cohabitation

The first point is that women, in general, have higher rates of neurotic illness than men. There is a large difference between married (15%) and cohabiting (24%) women. Among the men, on the other hand, there is no difference between those who are married and those who cohabit. Figure 8 shows anxiety and depressive disorders by marital status. Cohabiting women (133 per 1000) again have much higher rates than married women (86 per 1000), whereas cohabiting men (64 per 1000) have only slightly more anxiety and depression than their married (51 per 1000) counterparts. A close examination of the data presented in the table shows that cohabiting women are more irritable, worried, and depressed than married women. There is, however, no difference between married and cohabiting men in these symptoms. Note the large difference in irritability between men (18 %) and women (35%) who cohabit.

Neurotic symptoms by marital status for men and women

Percentage with significant symptoms

	Married		Cohabiting		Single	
	men	women	men	women	men	women
Irritability	19%	24%	18%	35%	19%	27%
Worry	16%	20%	20%	29%	16%	25%
Depression	8%	9%	8%	14%	9%	12%

It is significant that cohabiting women have a much worse neurotic profile than cohabiting men. The data suggest that the mental well-being of women is adversely affected by a cohabiting arrangement, whereas the mental well-being of men is hardly affected at all. Many women feel unhappy about a sexual relationship that lacks permanence. It seems likely that women are worried by the possibility that they may become pregnant, and then face the consequences with a man who is not their husband and has made no life-long commitment to the relationship.

7. Conclusion

So what conclusions can be drawn from the data? What advantages does cohabitation have over marriage? The idea that a cohabiting relationship is equivalent to marriage is clearly unfounded. The information presented above suggests a large difference in commitment between the two types of relationship. Cohabiting is characterised by a greater incidence of sexual unfaithfulness, with all its consequences. The higher levels of smoking probably indicate the stress that pregnant women experience in a cohabiting relationship. The high level of abortion is further evidence that those who cohabit are less committed to the idea of having children and raising a family. It is probable that cohabiting women sense this lack of commitment and therefore become stressed when they are pregnant, for they fear that they will, quite literally, be left holding the baby. It is also significant that cohabiting women have high levels of anxiety and depression, emphasising the unsatisfactory nature of the relationship from a woman's point of view. Without doubt, cohabiting has serious consequences for the health and well-being of all concerned in the relationship. In particular, cohabiting is bad for women and for any children that are born as a consequence. The evidence shows that marriage, as instituted by God, is better.

> *"Today the family is in serious crisis. If we fail to find a solution we will be plunged into a new dark age of lawlessness and chaos, which could destroy our civilisation."*
>
> MICHAEL HARPER

7.1 The Church needs to warn society

We have seen that marriage has been designed by God for the good of men, women and children. Yet contemporary society has made cohabitation socially acceptable, and there are few prepared to defend the Christian view of marriage.

7. Conclusion

The message that widespread cohabitation can do great damage to society is seldom heard and it is unfashionable to point out that those who cohabit are harming themselves, for they have entered a relationship that is contrary to biblical truth and therefore not pleasing to God. We believe that society is in desperate need of the biblical view of marriage. The Christian Church has a duty to reaffirm these truths and to warn society and individuals of the dangers of disobeying God's law. Many people are ignorant of what the Bible teaches about marriage. The Church, as the light of the world, has a duty to point people in the right direction. Cohabitation is wrong: it is against God's law, and is morally indefensible. The Church should not hesitate to say so – indeed, the Church has an obligation to speak out.

7.2 An invitation to a better way

We have seen that those who cohabit lose by not exchanging vows in accordance with the pattern designed for us by God. Those who cohabit before marriage do themselves and their partners a disservice. They run the risk of losing their self respect and becoming devalued as human beings. It is far better for a couple who are in love to wait until they have made their marriage vows before they live together. Real love is not selfish but is patient and will be prepared to wait. While recognising that some couples have lived in a stable cohabiting relationship for many years, we urge those involved to re-examine their relationship in the light of biblical truth. We know that the God who instituted marriage is also the God of grace who can forgive and restore all those who come to Him.

> *"There is no more lovely, friendly or charming relationship, communion or company, than a good marriage."*
>
> MARTIN LUTHER

7. Conclusion

7.3 Good news for those who cohabit

The essence of the Christian gospel is salvation. Christ came to seek and save those who are lost. As he said, *"For I have not come to call the righteous, but sinners"* (Matthew 9: 13). This call includes all humankind, for all have sinned. So the Christian message is one of hope for sinful people. Christ, when dealing with the woman who was caught in adultery, asked those among her accusers who were without sin to cast the first stone. None could do so, for all had sinned. He said to her, *"Neither do I condemn you. Go and sin no more"* (John 8: 1-11). So while Christ clearly disapproved of her action, he offered her forgiveness and salvation. This is the good news for those who find themselves in a cohabiting relationship. The Christian gospel welcomes them, offering forgiveness and hope of a better life. Christ can heal the broken-hearted, and repair imperfect human relationships. Marriage, not cohabitation, is the better way.

> *"The nearer a nation's laws about marriage approach the law of Christ, the higher has the moral tone of that nation always proved to be."*
>
> J C RYLE

Bibliography

1. Trends in marriage and cohabitation: the decline in marriage and the changing pattern of living in partnership. John Haskey. *Population Trends 80;* OPCS. HMSO (London 1995).

2. *General Household Survey* 1993 (Series GHS No.24); OPCS. HMSO (London 1995).

3. *Sexual Attitudes and Lifestyles.* Blackwell Scientific Publications; 1994: Oxford. Chapter 5; Anne Johnson and Jane Wadsworth.

4. Premarital cohabitation and the probability of subsequent divorce: Analysis using new data from the General Household Survey. John Haskey. *Population Trends 68;* OPCS. HMSO (London 1992).

5. Smoking prevalence among school children and pregnant women. Health in Croydon 1994/5 *The Annual Report of the Director of Public Health.*

6. *Mortality statistics 1991 – perinatal and infant: social and biological factors* (Series DH3 No.25); OPCS. HMSO (London 1993).

7. *Surveys of Psychiatric Morbidity in Great Britain; Report 1.* The prevalence of psychiatric morbidity among adults living in private households. OPCS. HMSO (London 1995).

8. Sexual relations and marriage. *Care Family Booklets.* Care 1994.

9. *Pastoral Ethics.* David Atkinson. Lynx Communications 1994.

10. *Independent on Sunday.* 18 August 1996, quoting High Court Judge Brenda Hoggett.

Acknowledgments

All scriptures references are from the Holy Bible,
New International Version. Copyright 1973, 1978, 1984 by
the International Bible Society. Used by permission.

John Haskey, from Trends in marriage and cohabitation: the decline in marriage and the
changing pattern of living in partnership. Population Trends 80; OPCS. London

Archbishop Dr George Carey, from his speech "Valuing families in church and society";
General Synod, 30 November 1995. London. Used by permission

John Calvin, from John Calvin's Sermons on Ephesians
The Banner of Truth Trust. Edinburgh. Used by permission

Henri Blocher, from In the Beginning by Henri Blocher
Inter-Varsity Press. Leicester. Used by permission

John Stott, from Issues Facing Christian's Today
Marshall Pickering, part of Harper Collins Publishers. London. Used by permission

Anne Johnson and Jane Wadsworth, from; Sexual Attitudes and Lifestyles
Blackwell Scientific Publications; 1994. Oxford. Used by permission

Lewis Smedes, from Mere Morality
Eerdmans Publishing Co. Grand Rapids, USA. Used by permission

William Barclay, from Ethics in a Permissive Society
Fontana Books 1971. Used by permission

Michael Harper, from Equal and Different
Hodder and Stoughton Ltd, Hodder Headline PLC. London. Used by permission

Derek Prince, from The Marriage Covenant
Derek Prince Ministries – International, Whitaker House, Springdale, PA USA.
Used by permission

Martin Luther, quoted from Dictionary of Religious Quotations by Margaret Pepper.
Andre Deutsch. London

J C Ryle, quoted from More Gathered Gold by John Blanchard
Evangelical Press 1986

BELMONT HOUSE PUBLISHING

Published by Belmont House Publishing
36 The Crescent, Belmont, Sutton, Surrey. SM2 6BJ England

Printed by R.Young & Son

© 1997 Declan Flanagan and Dr Ted Williams
First published in 1997

ISBN 0 9529939 0 2

A CIP catalogue record of this book is available
from the British Library